# Pareto Analysis

Date: _____

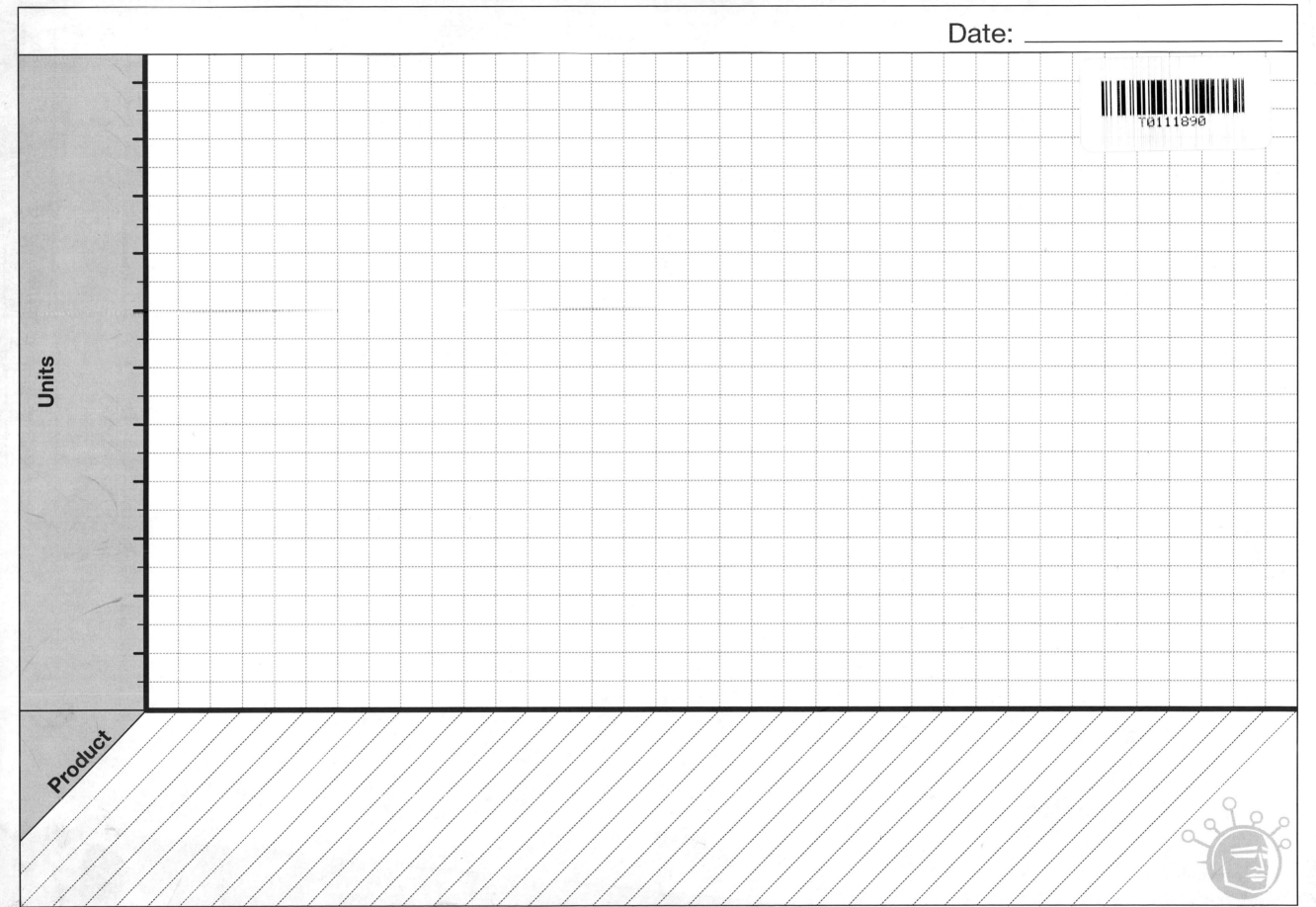

Units

Product

# areto An lysis

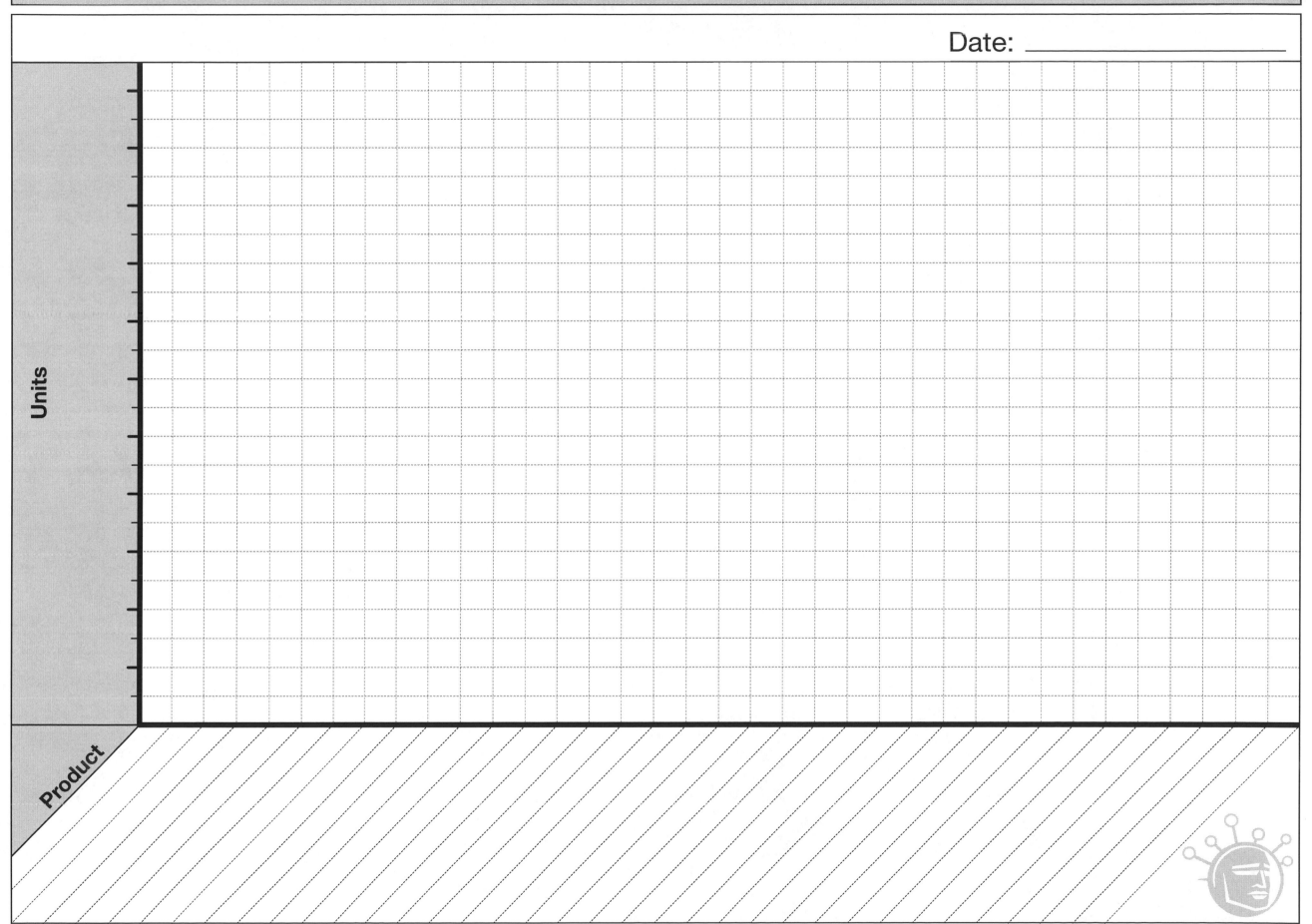

Date: _____

Units

Product

www.enna.com
www.productivitypress.com

# Pareto Analysis

Date: _____

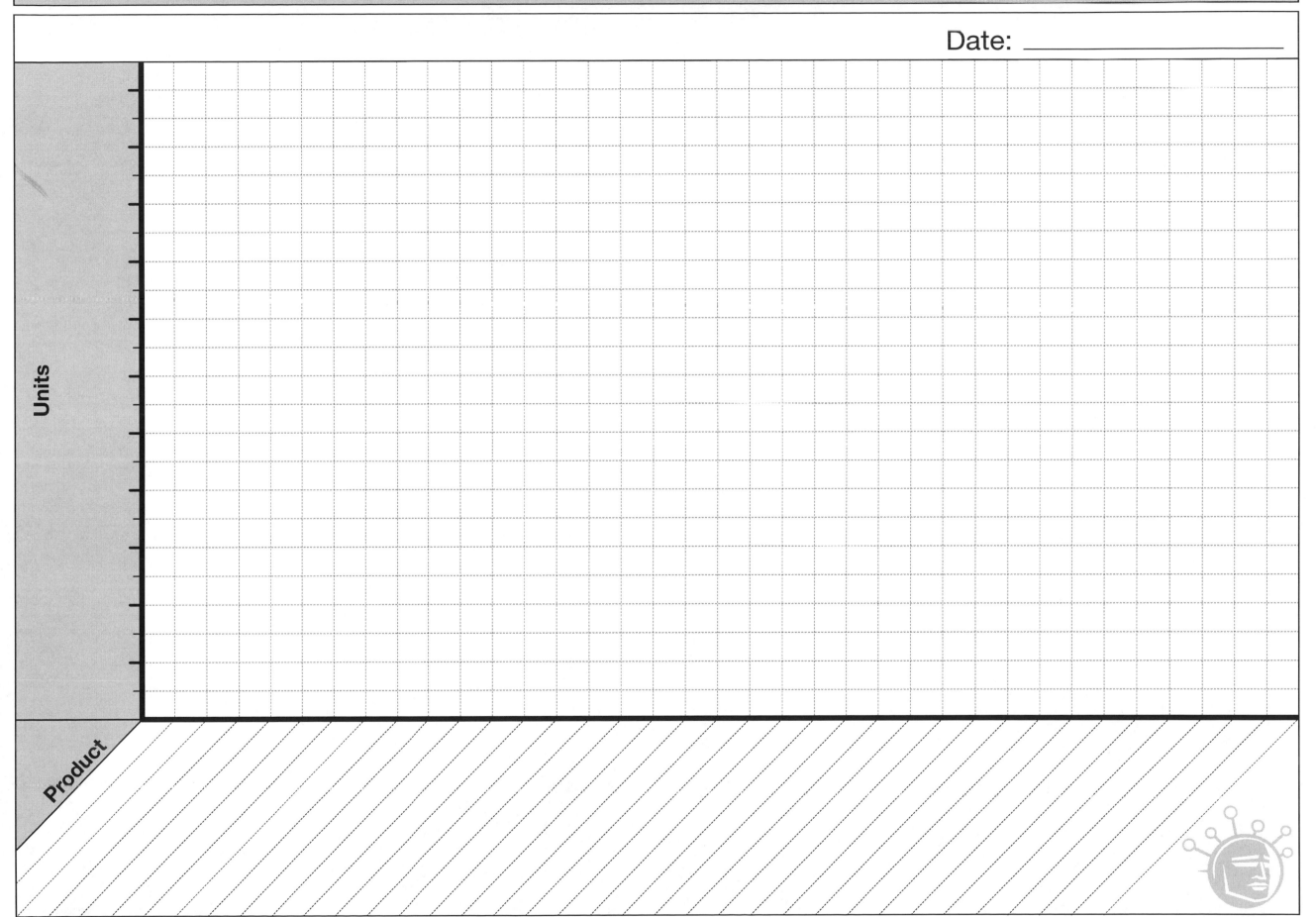

Units

Product

# areto An lysis

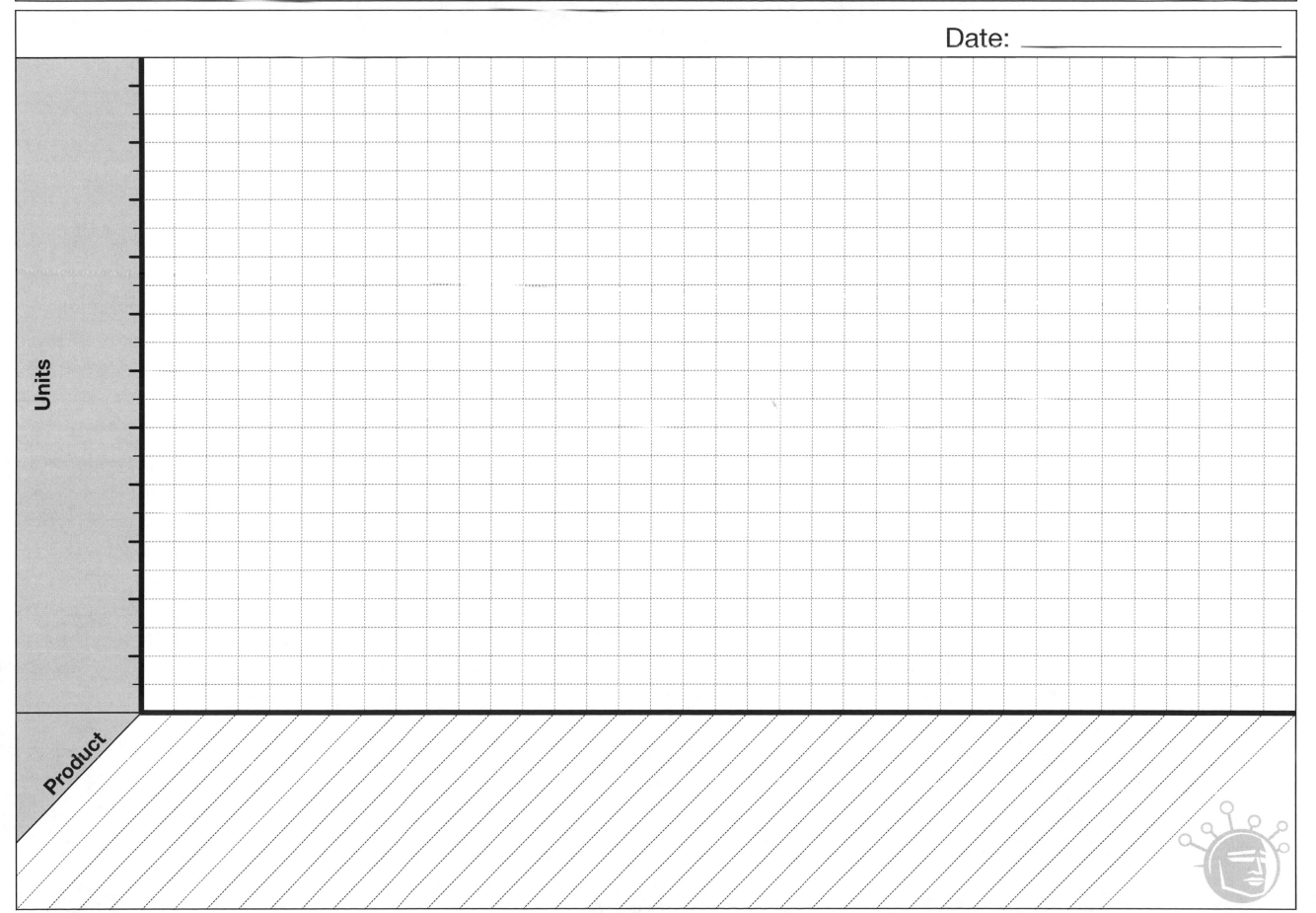

Date: _____

Units

Product

www.enna.com
www.productivitypress.com

# Pareto Analysis

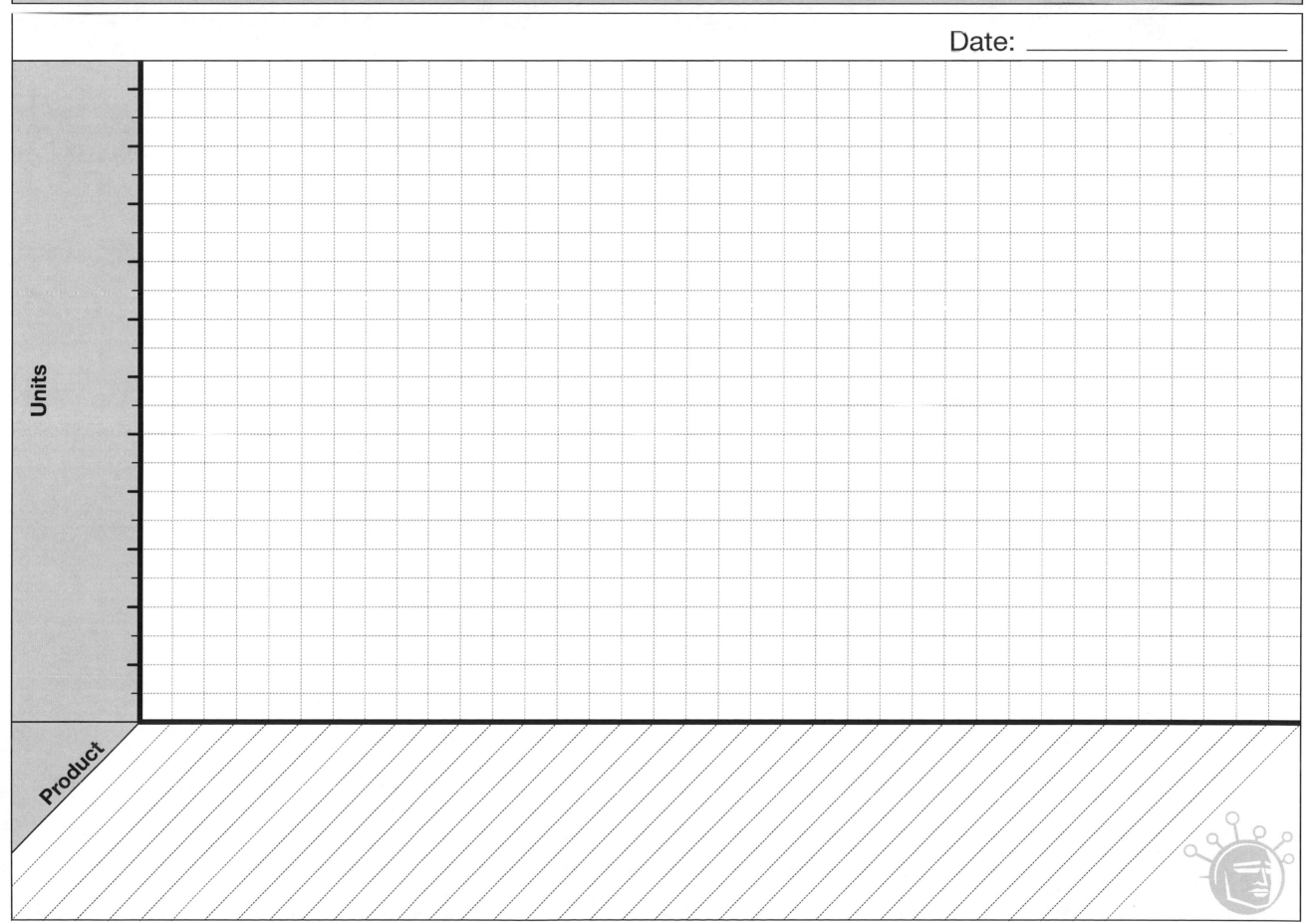

Date: _____

Units

Product

A **Productivity Press** Product

# areto An lysis

Date: _____

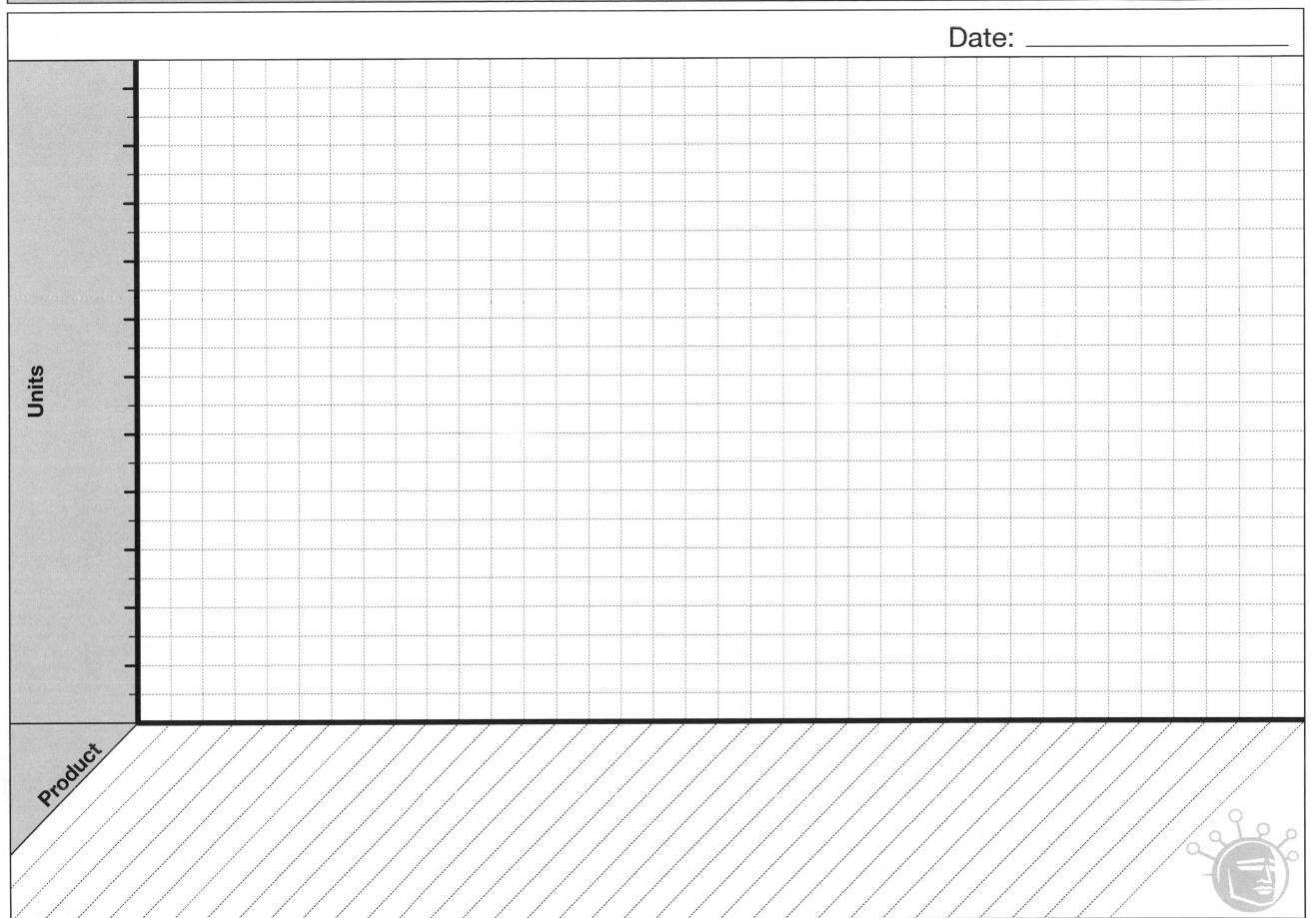

Units

Product

# Pareto Analysis

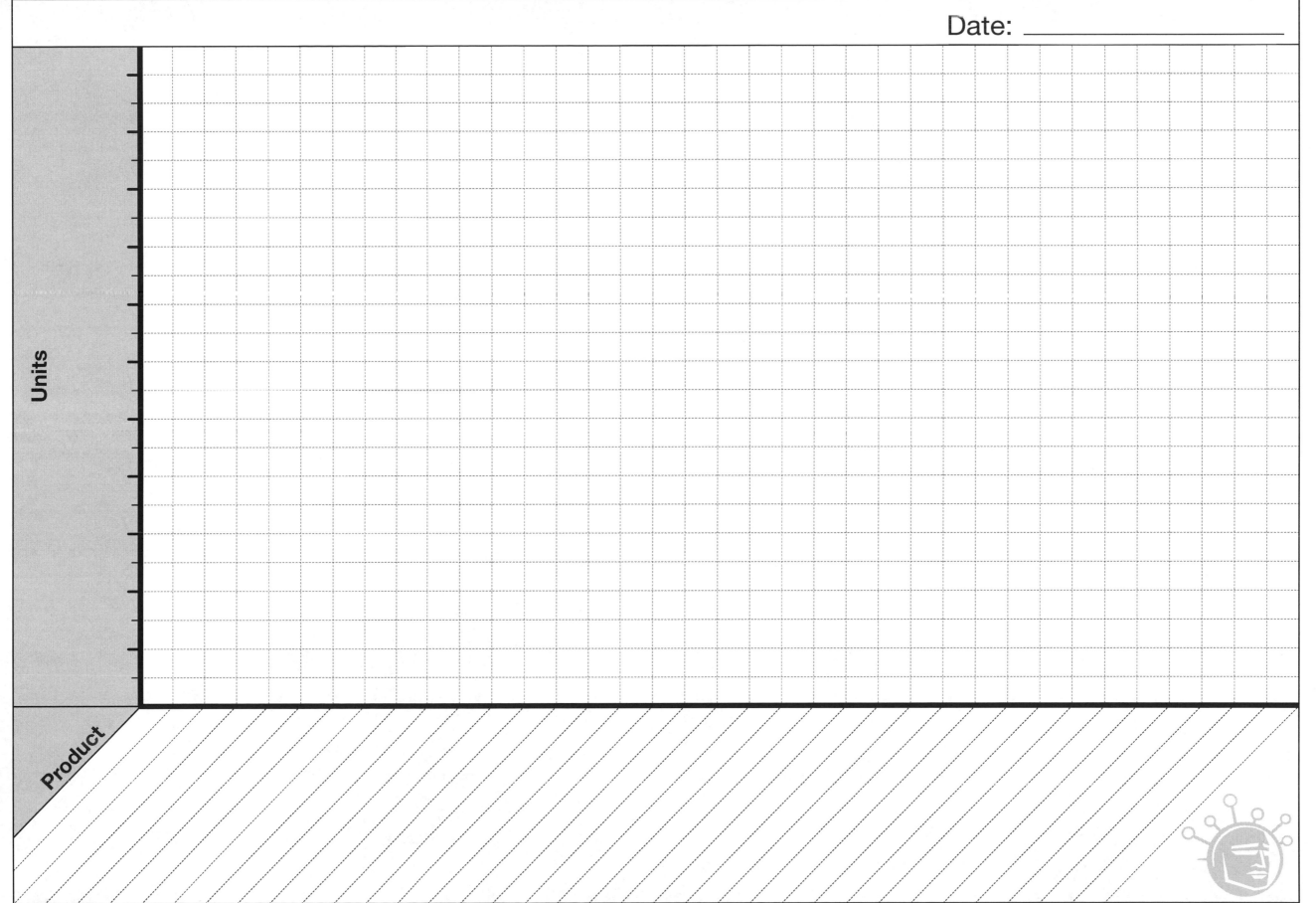

Date: _____

Units

Product

# Pareto Analysis

Date: _____

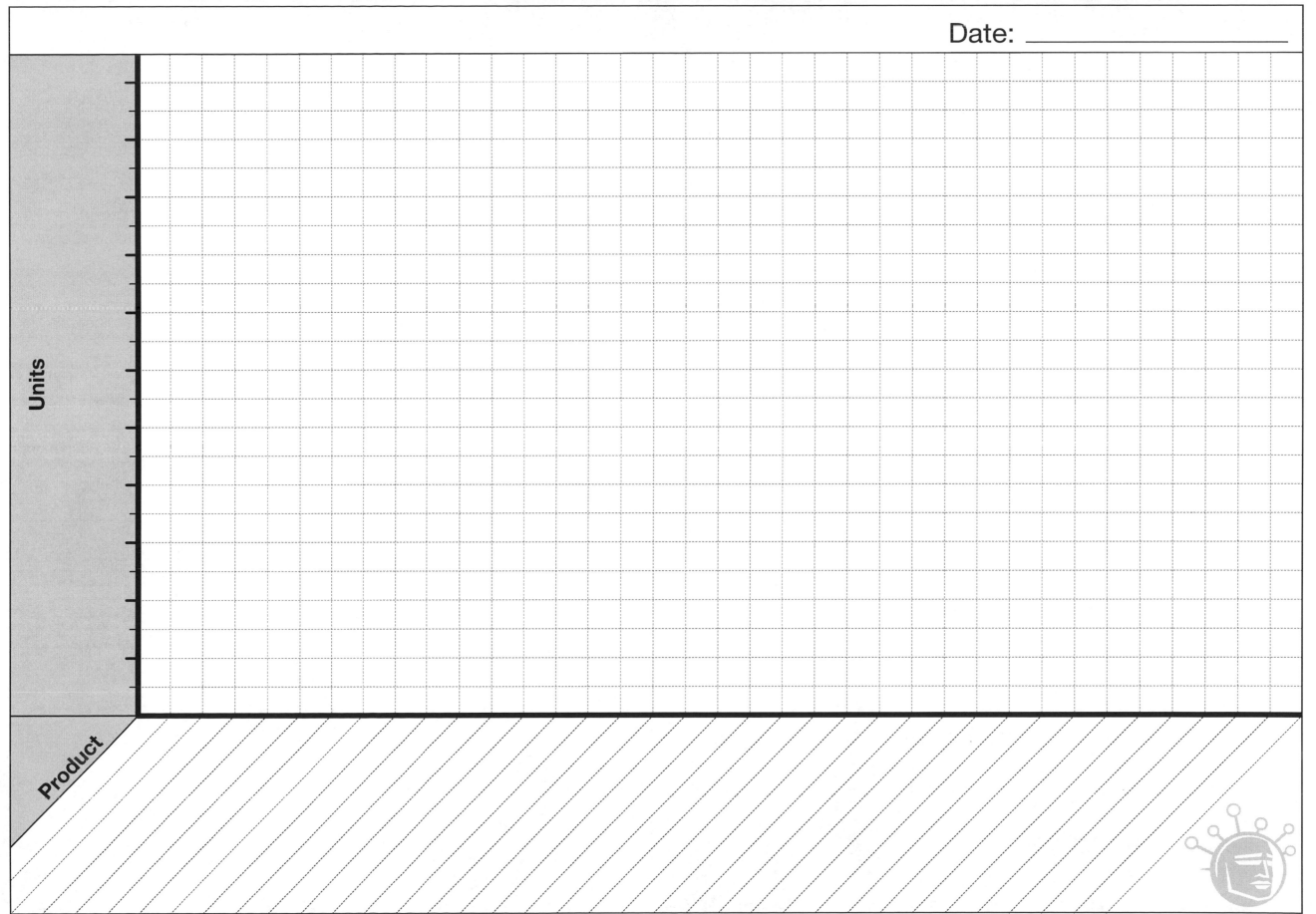

Units

Product

# areto An lysis

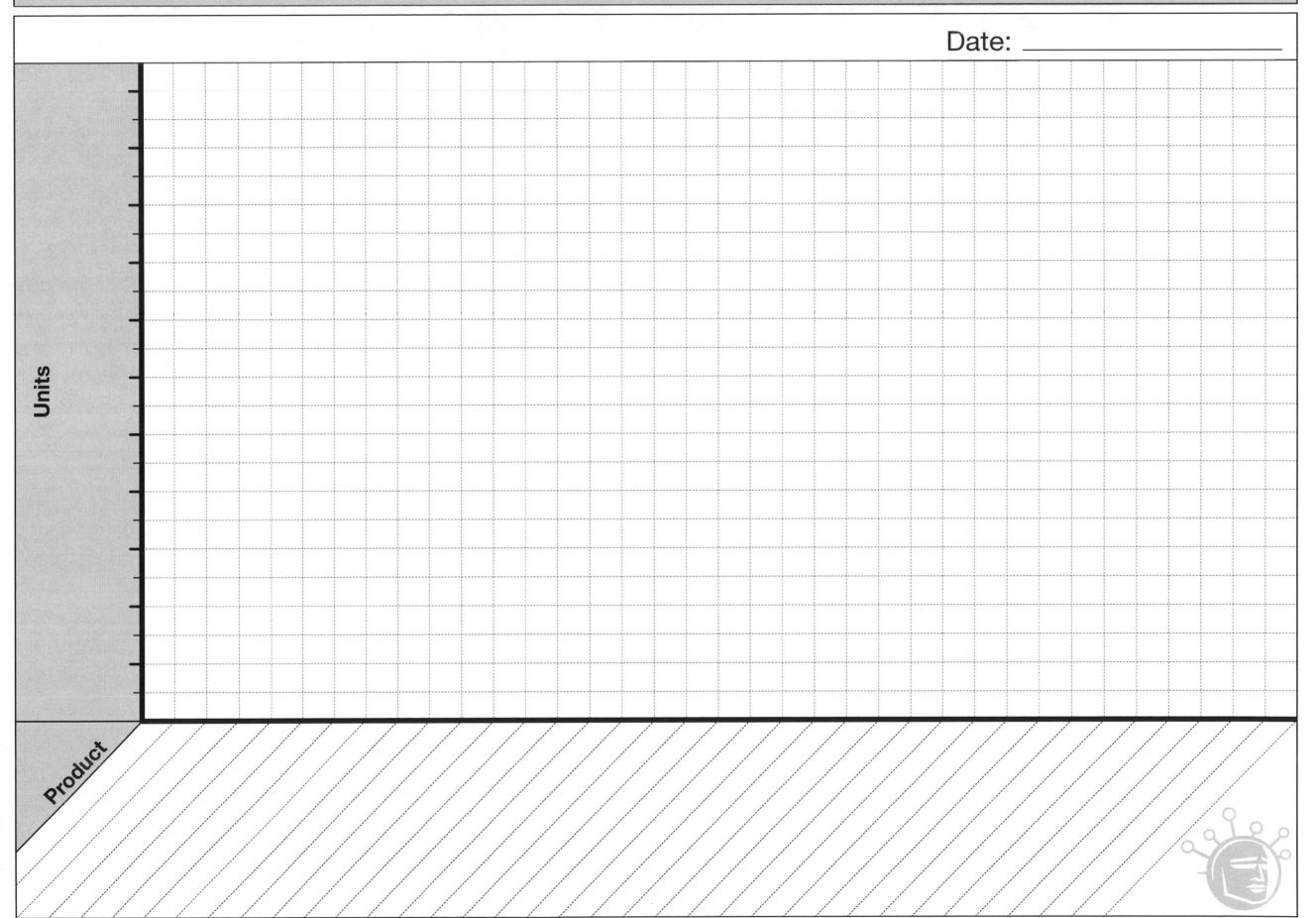

Date: _____

Units

Product

# areto An lysis

Date: _____

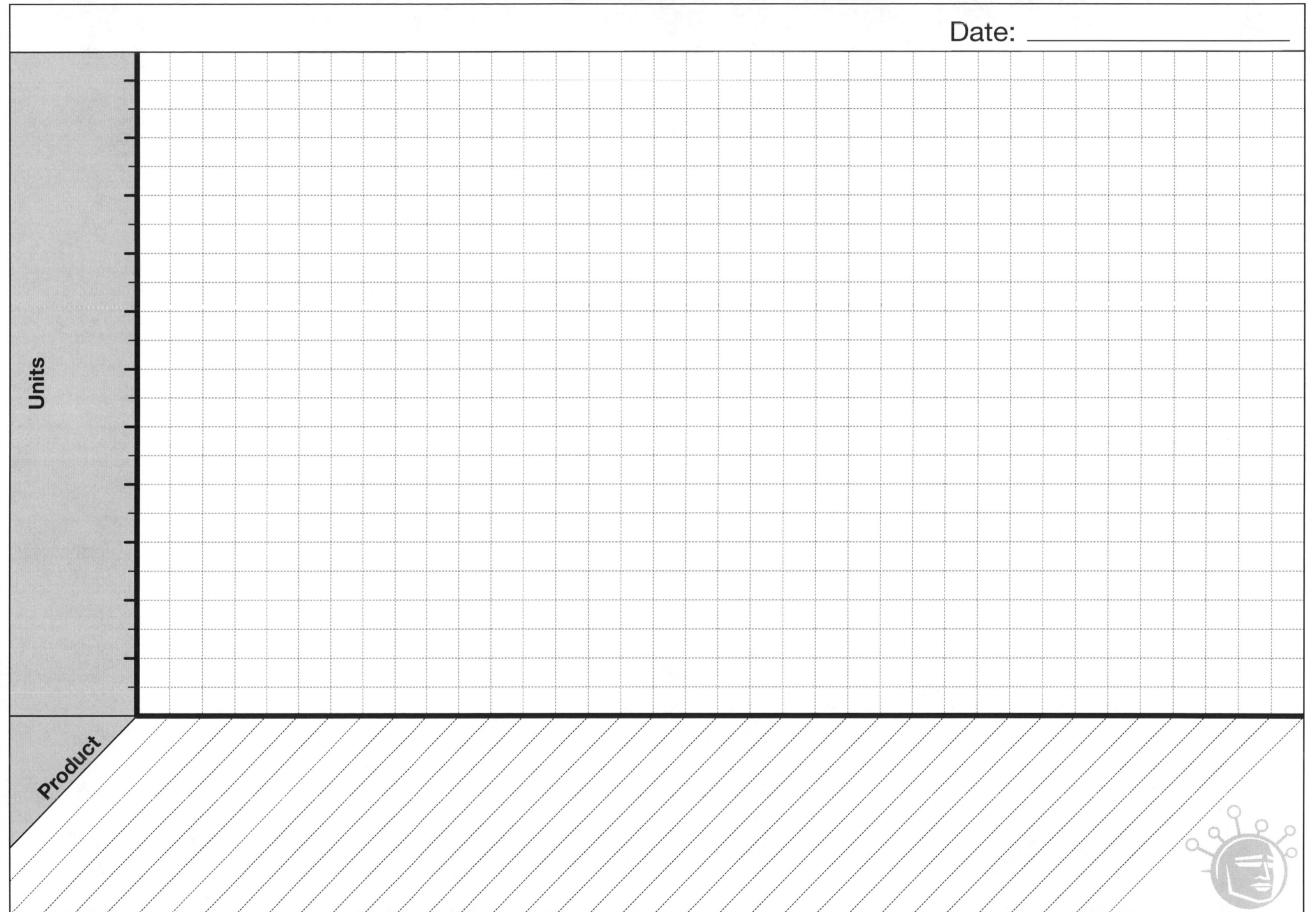

Units

Product

A **Productivity Press** Product

www.enna.com
www.productivitypress.com

# areto An lysis

Date: _____

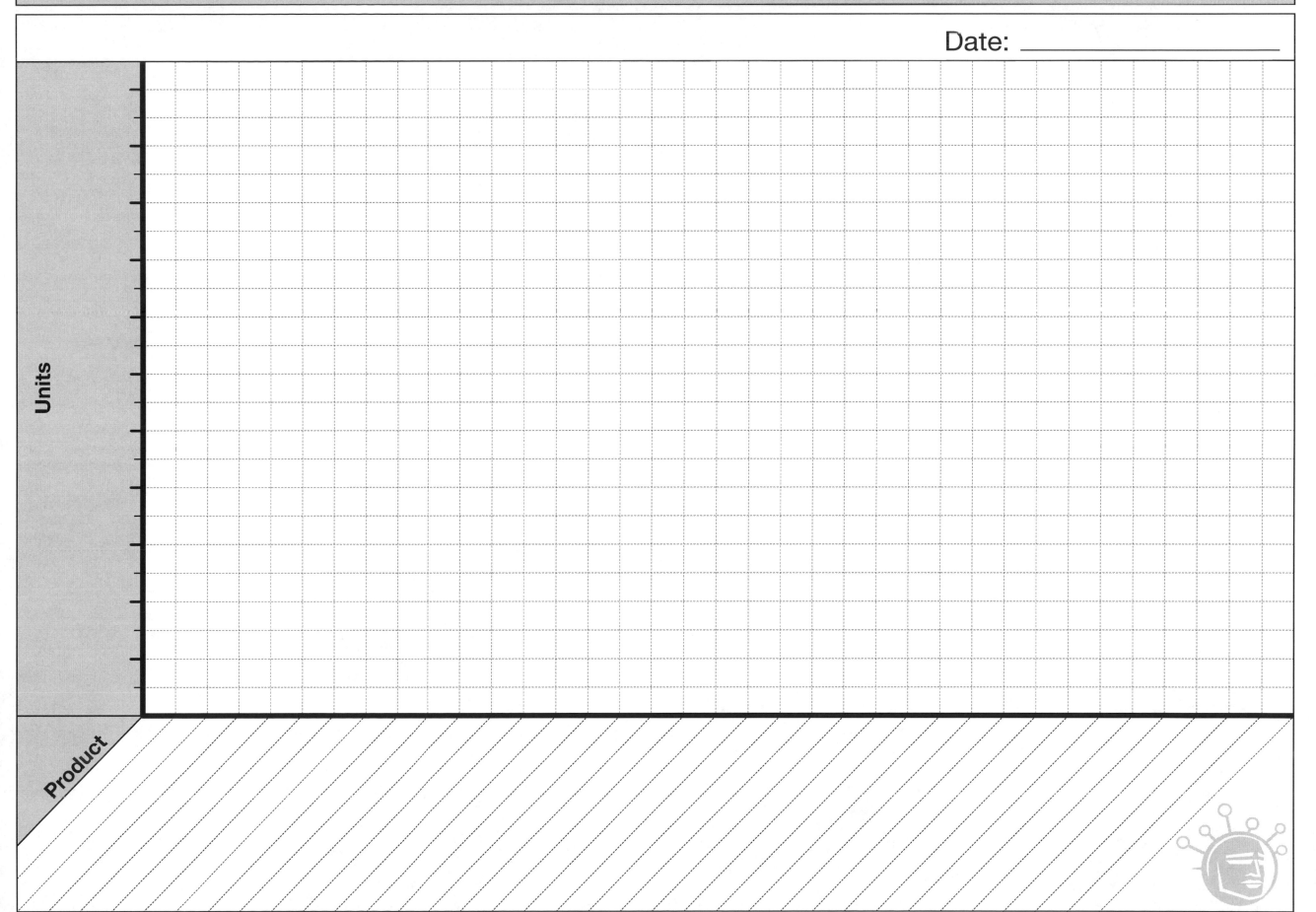

Units

Product

# areto An lysis

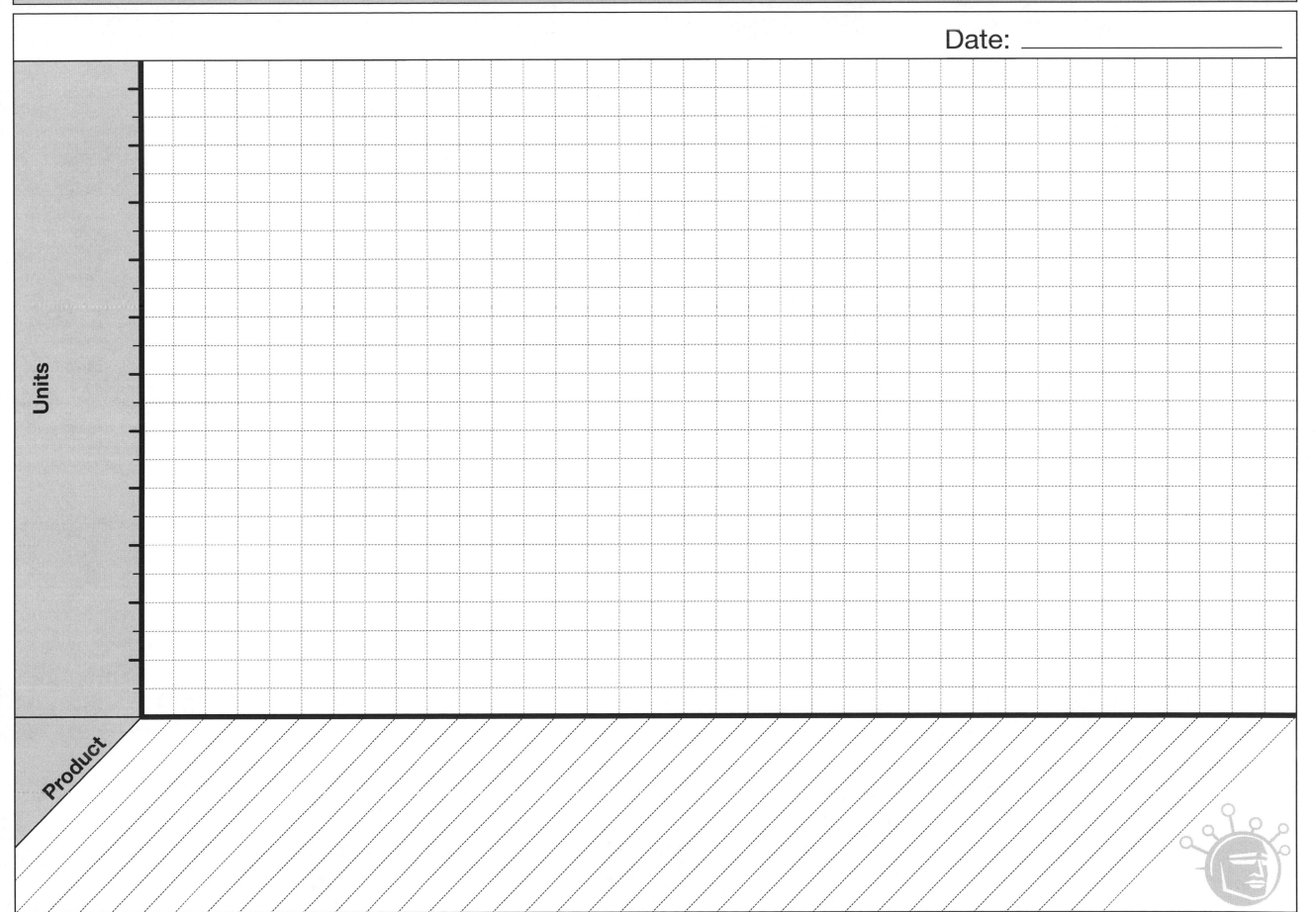

Date: _____

Units

Product

A **Productivity Press** Product

# areto An lysis

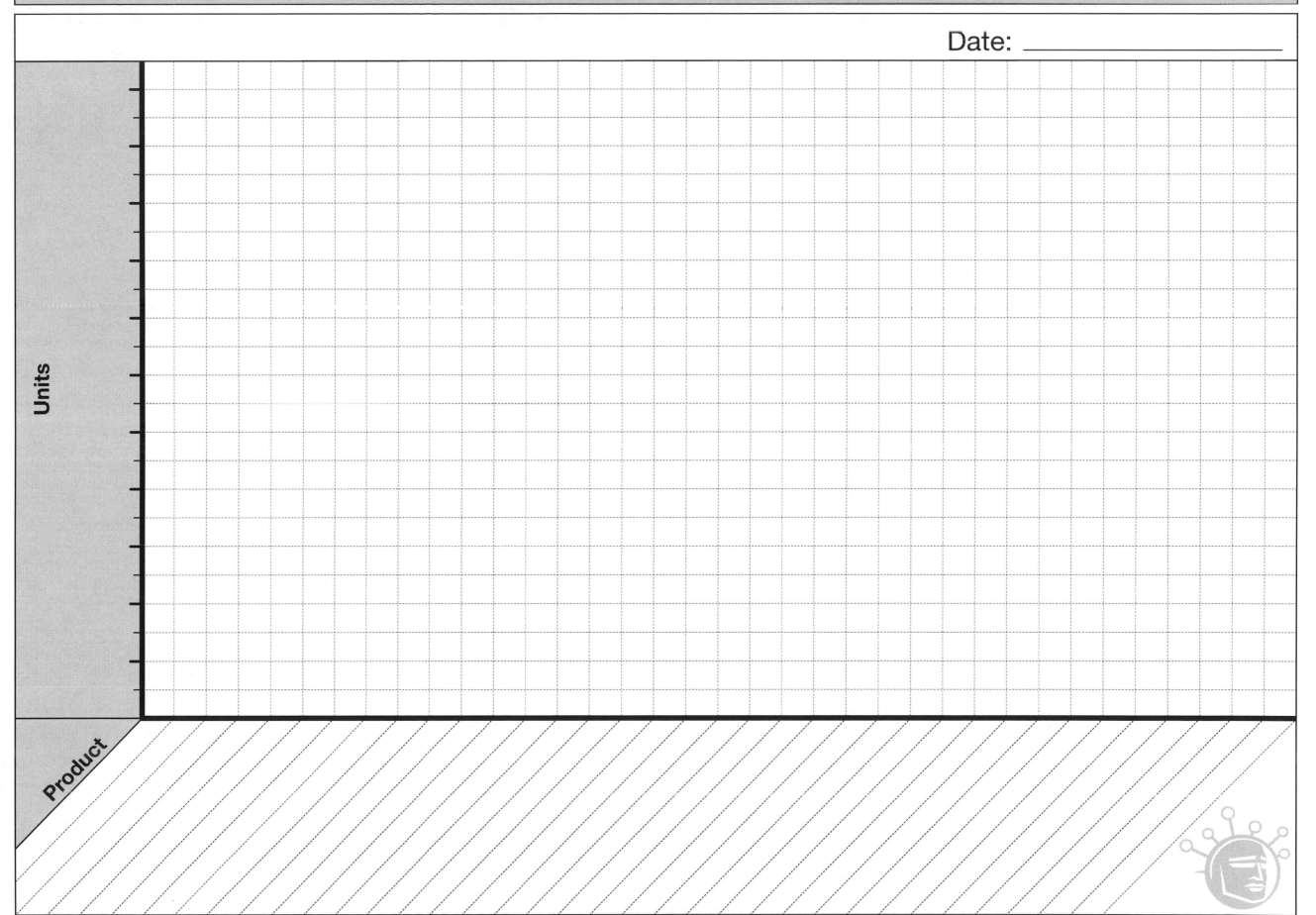

Date: _____

Units

Product

# areto An lysis

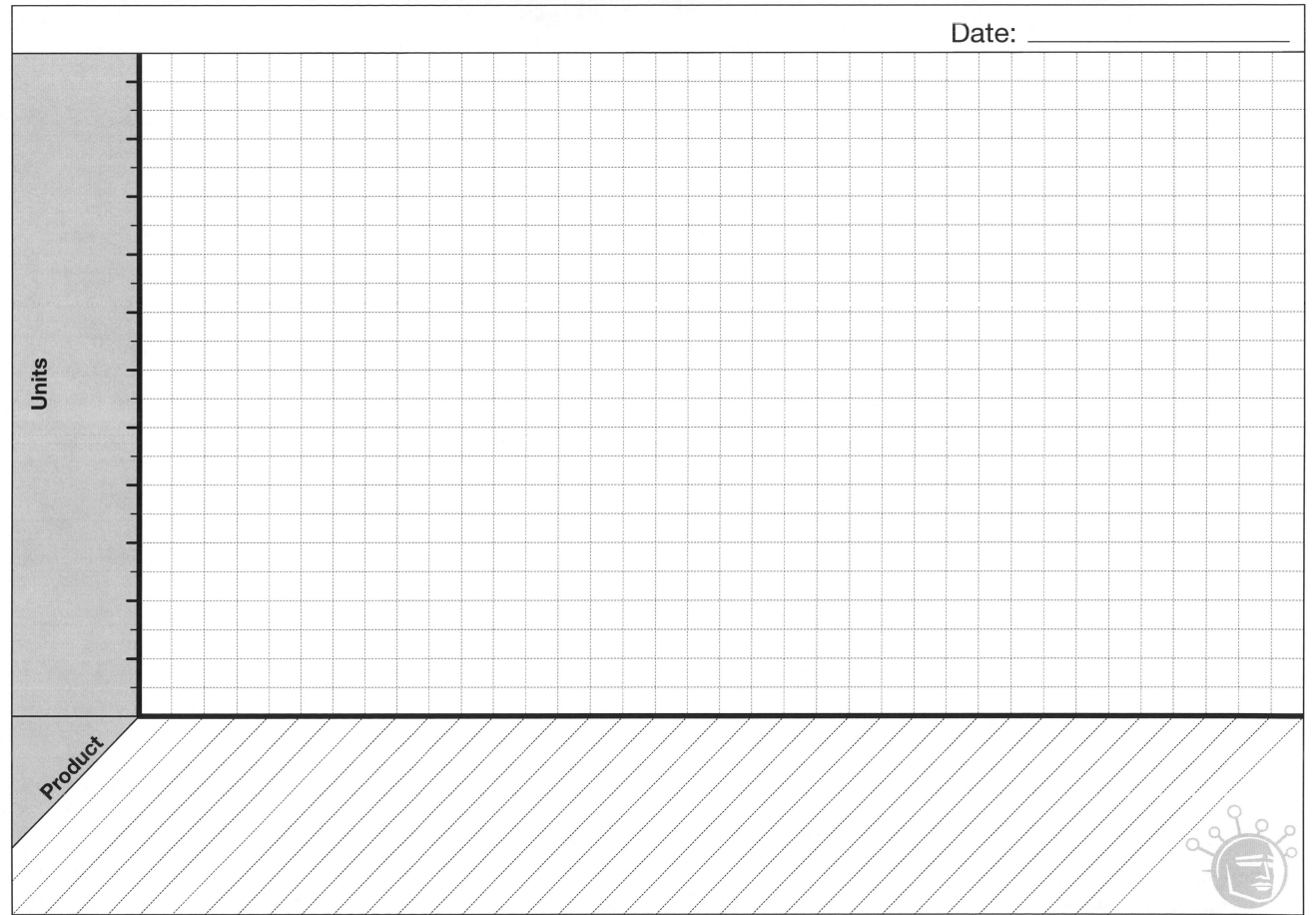

Date: _____

Units

Product

A **Productivity Press** Product

www.enna.com
www.productivitypress.com

# Pareto Analysis

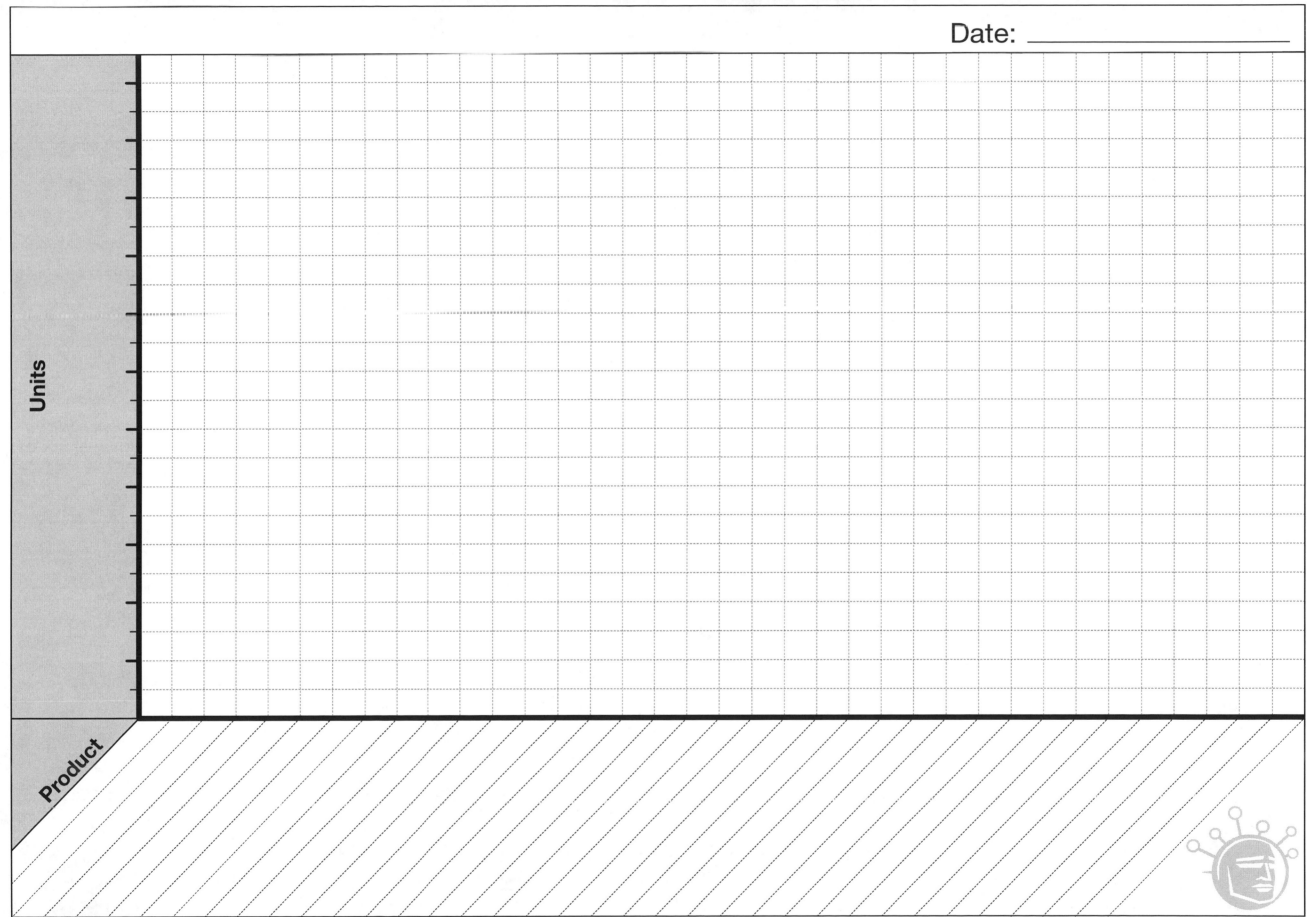

Date: _____

Units

Product

A **Productivity Press** Product

# Pareto Analysis

Date: _____

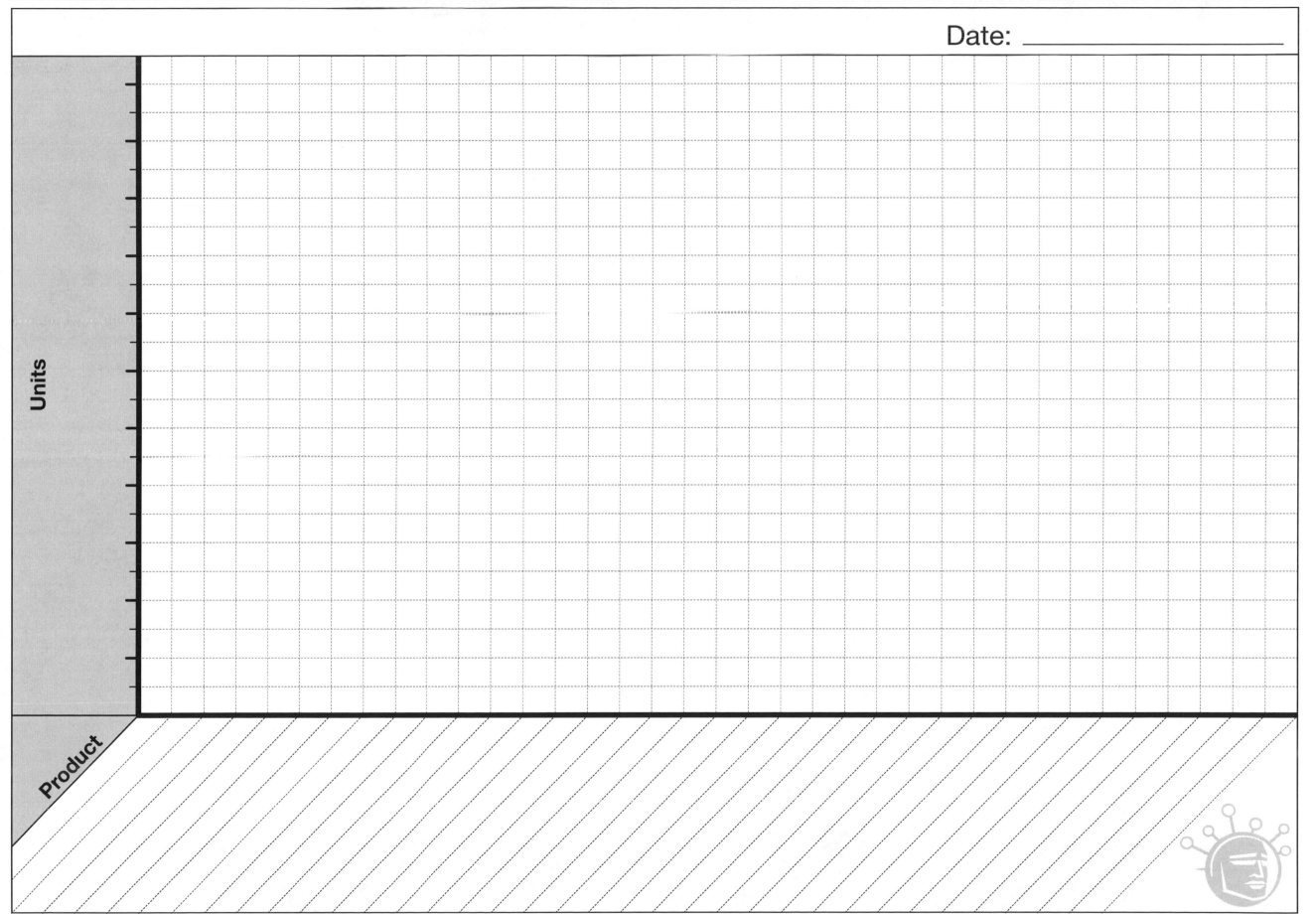

Units

Product

A **Productivity Press** Product

Date: _____

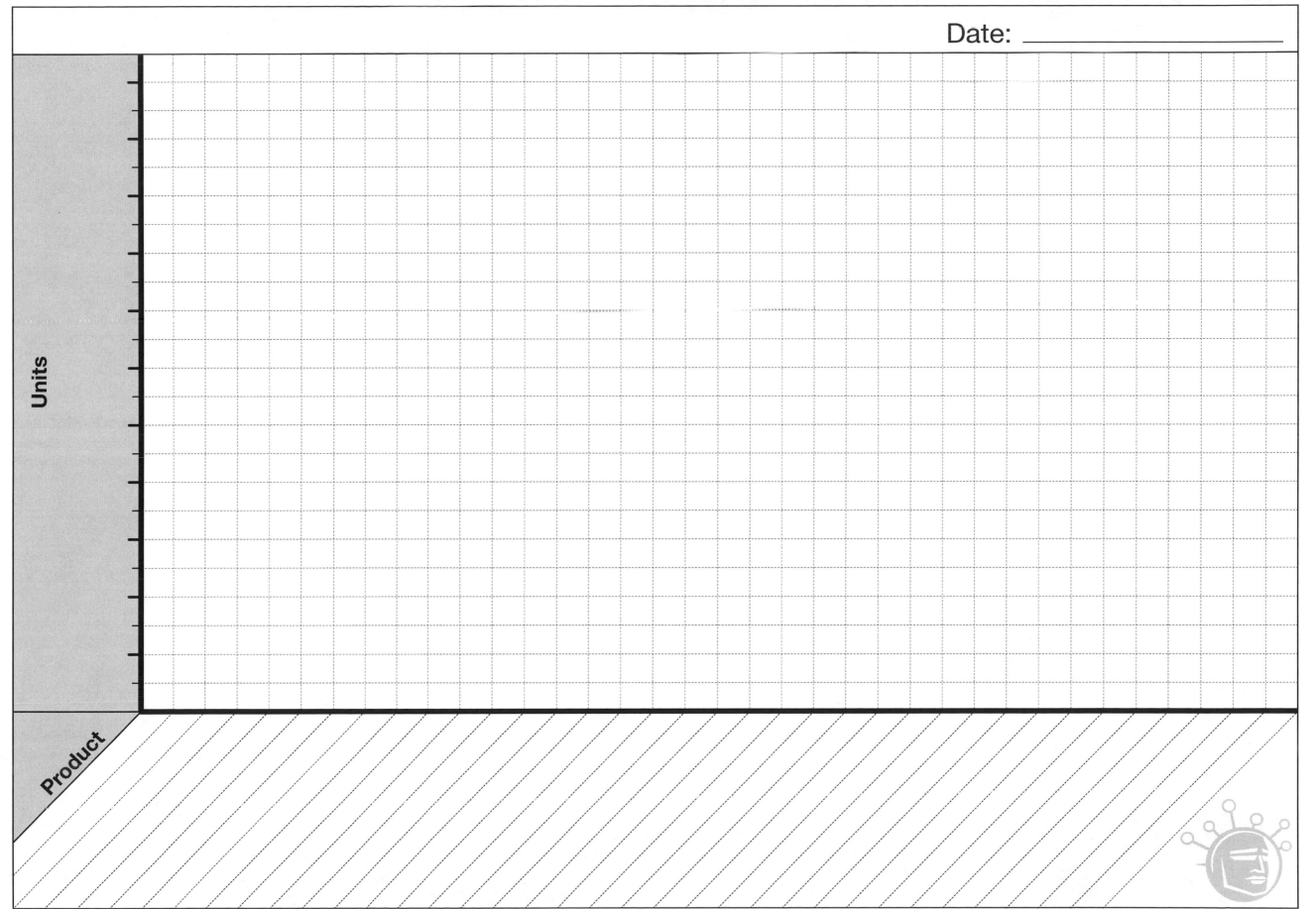

Units

Product

www.enna.com
www.productivitypress.com

# Pareto Analysis

Date: _____

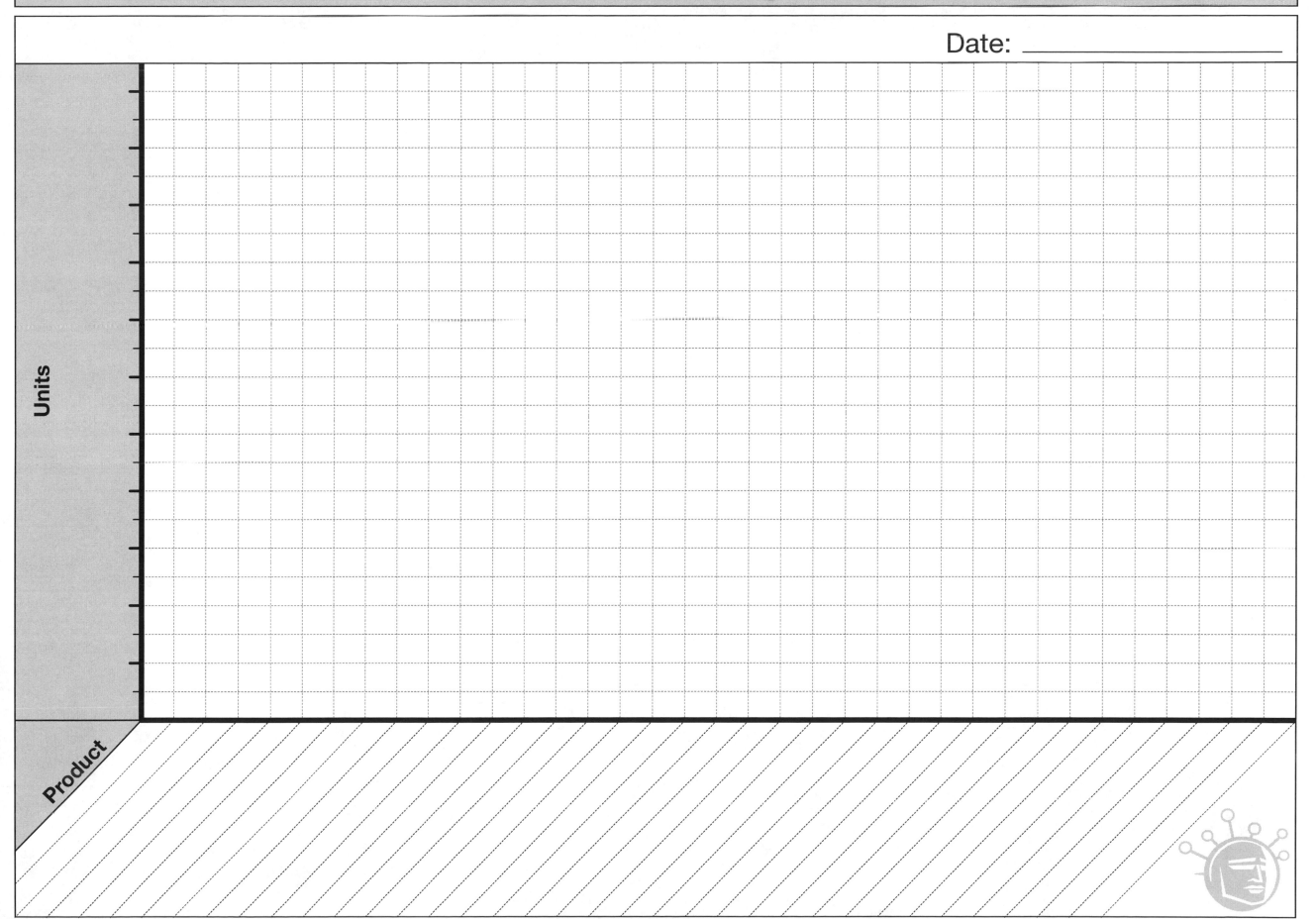

**Units**

**Product**

www.enna.com
www.productivitypress.com

# areto An lysis

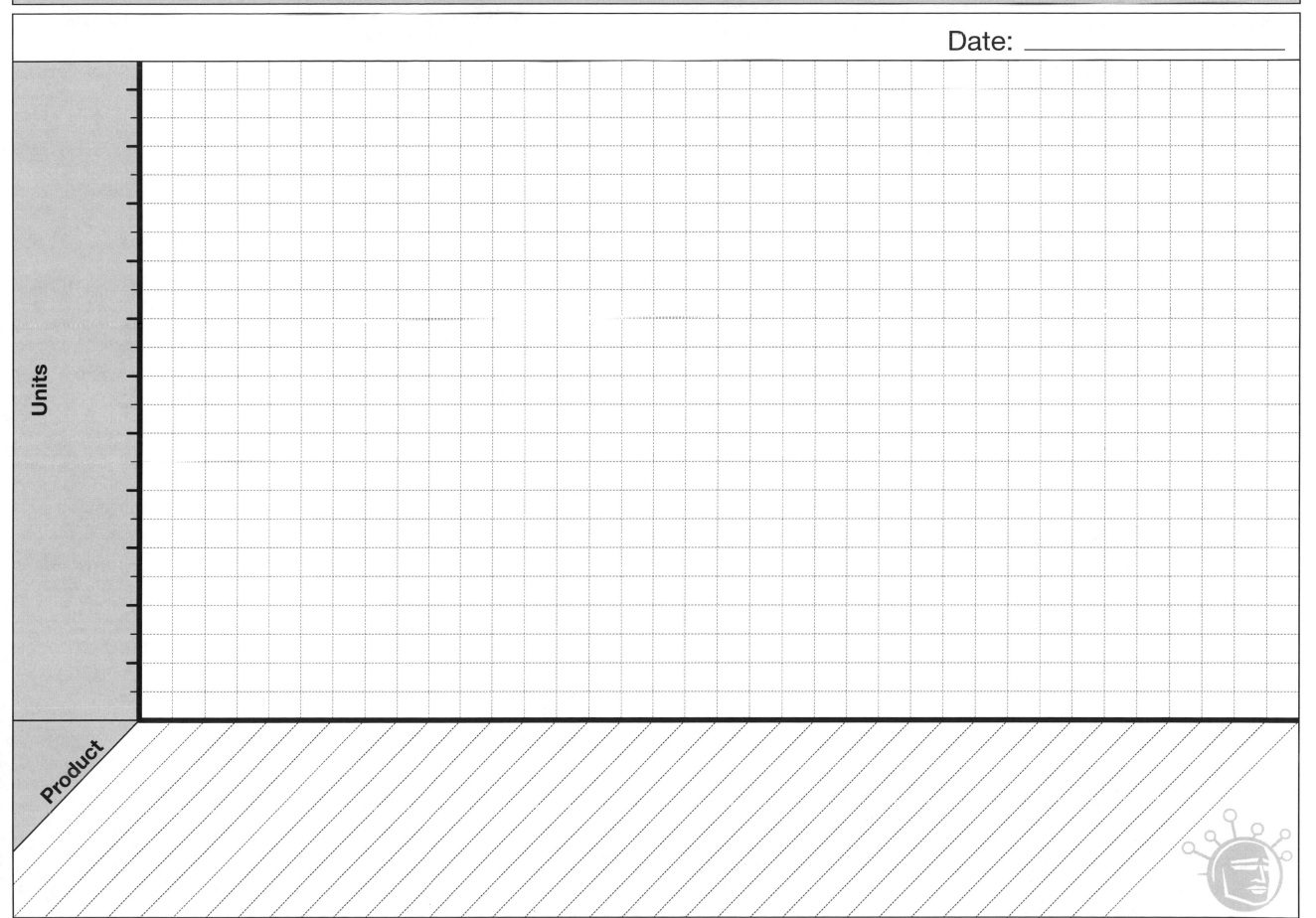

Date: _____

Units

Product

A **Productivity Press** Product

# areto An lysis

Date: _____

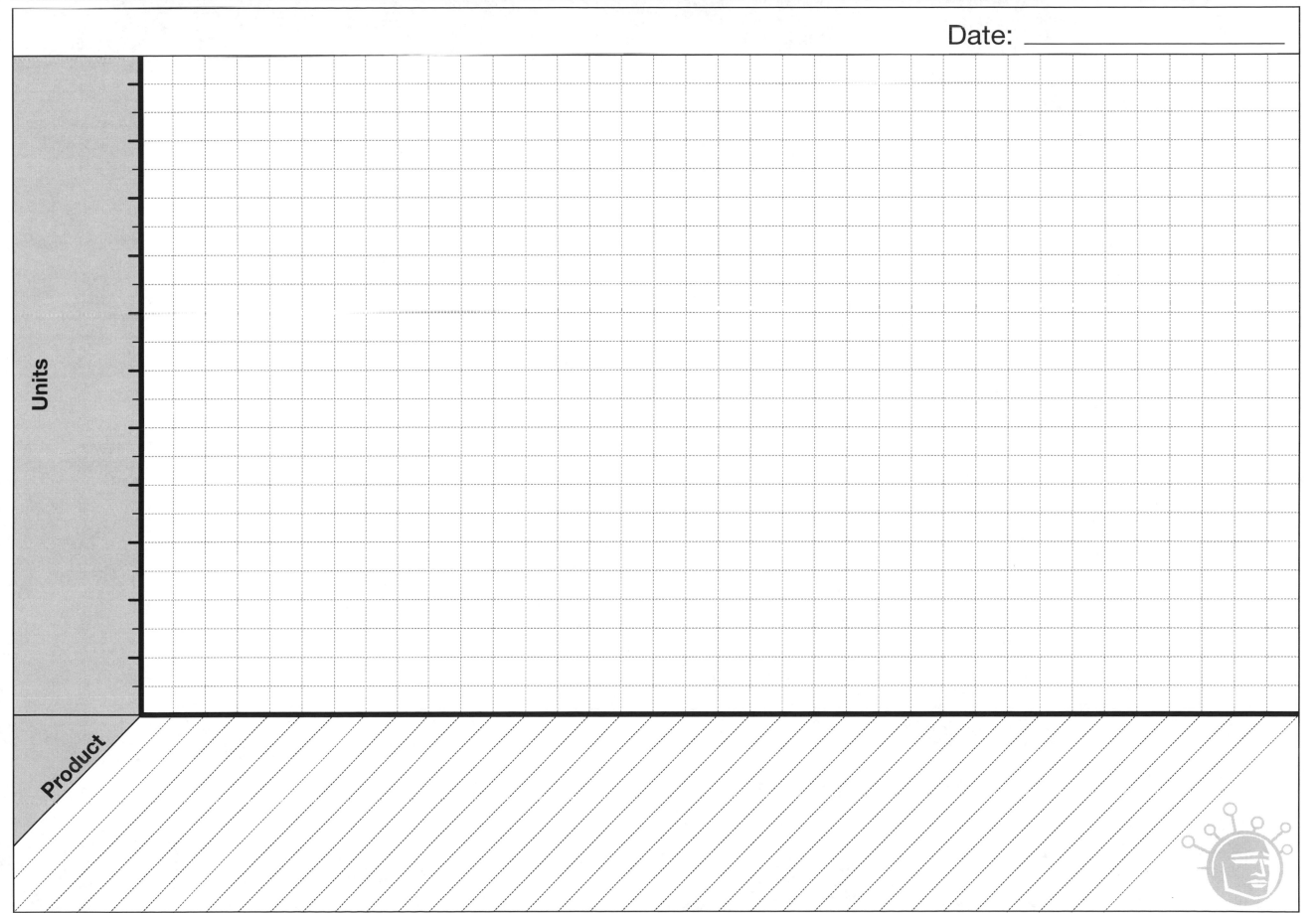

Units

Product

# areto An lysis

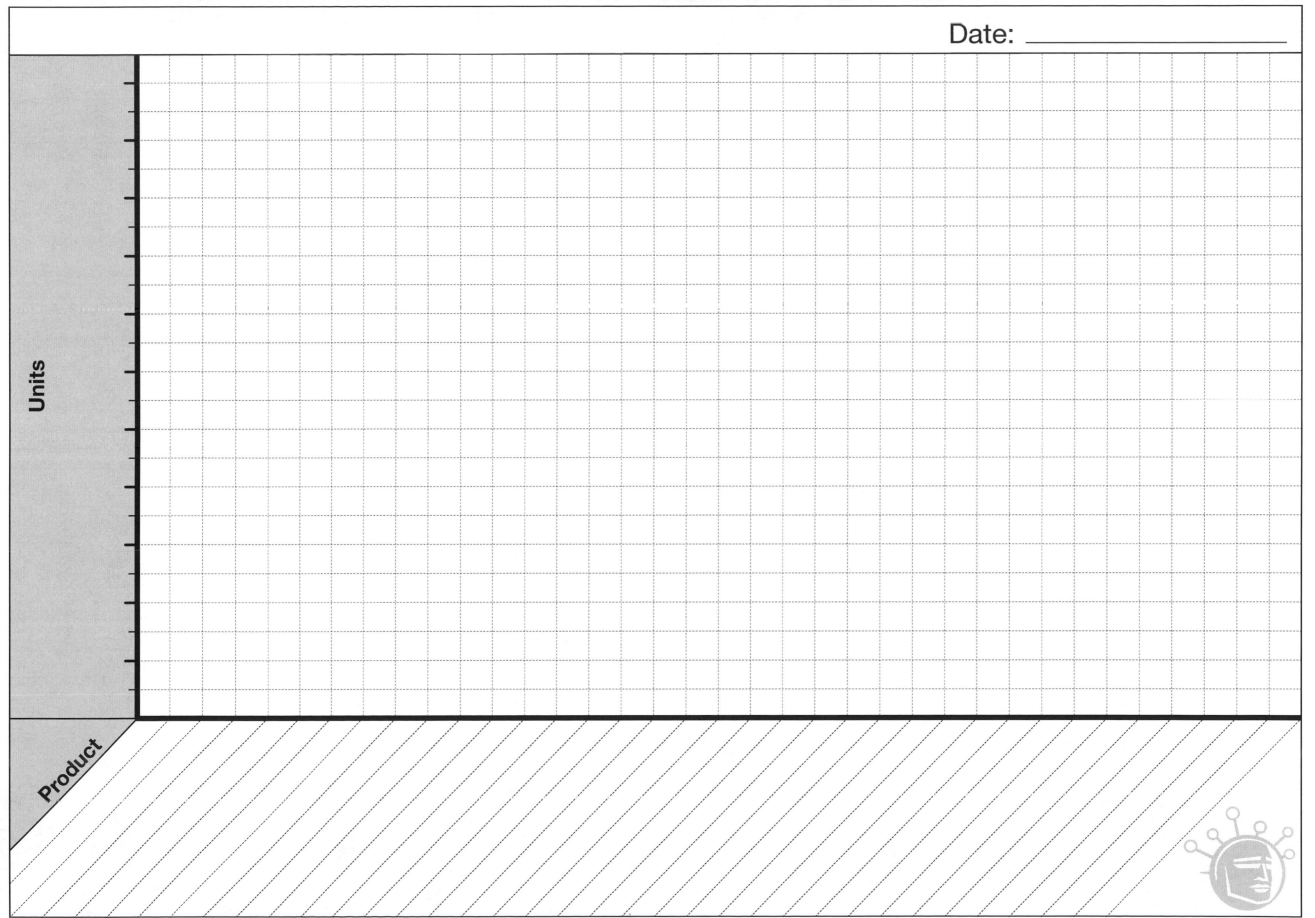

Date: _____

Units

Product

# ... r to An lysis

Date: _____

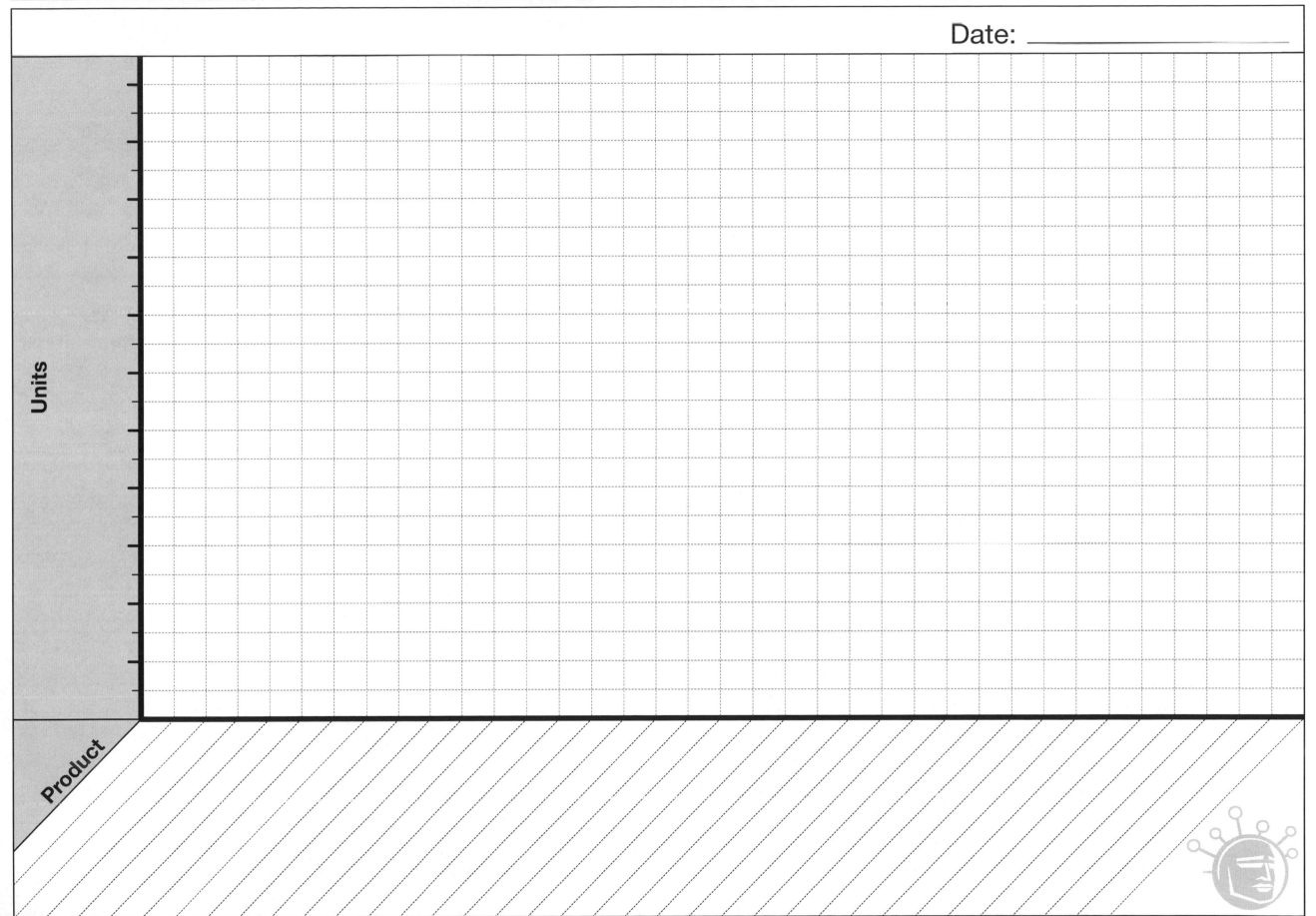

**Units**

**Product**

# Pareto Analysis

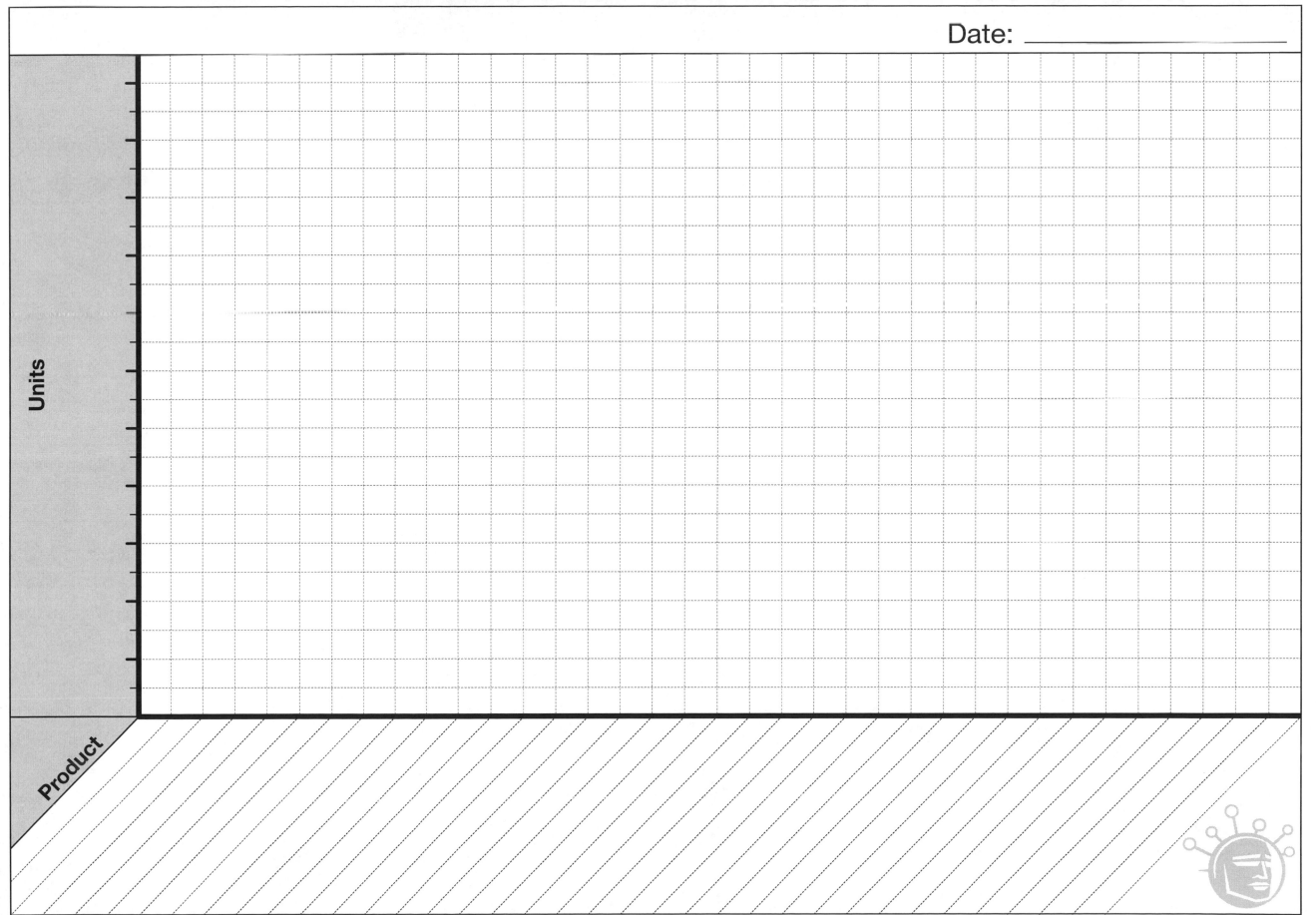

Date: _____

Units

Product

www.enna.com
www.productivitypress.com

# areto An lysis

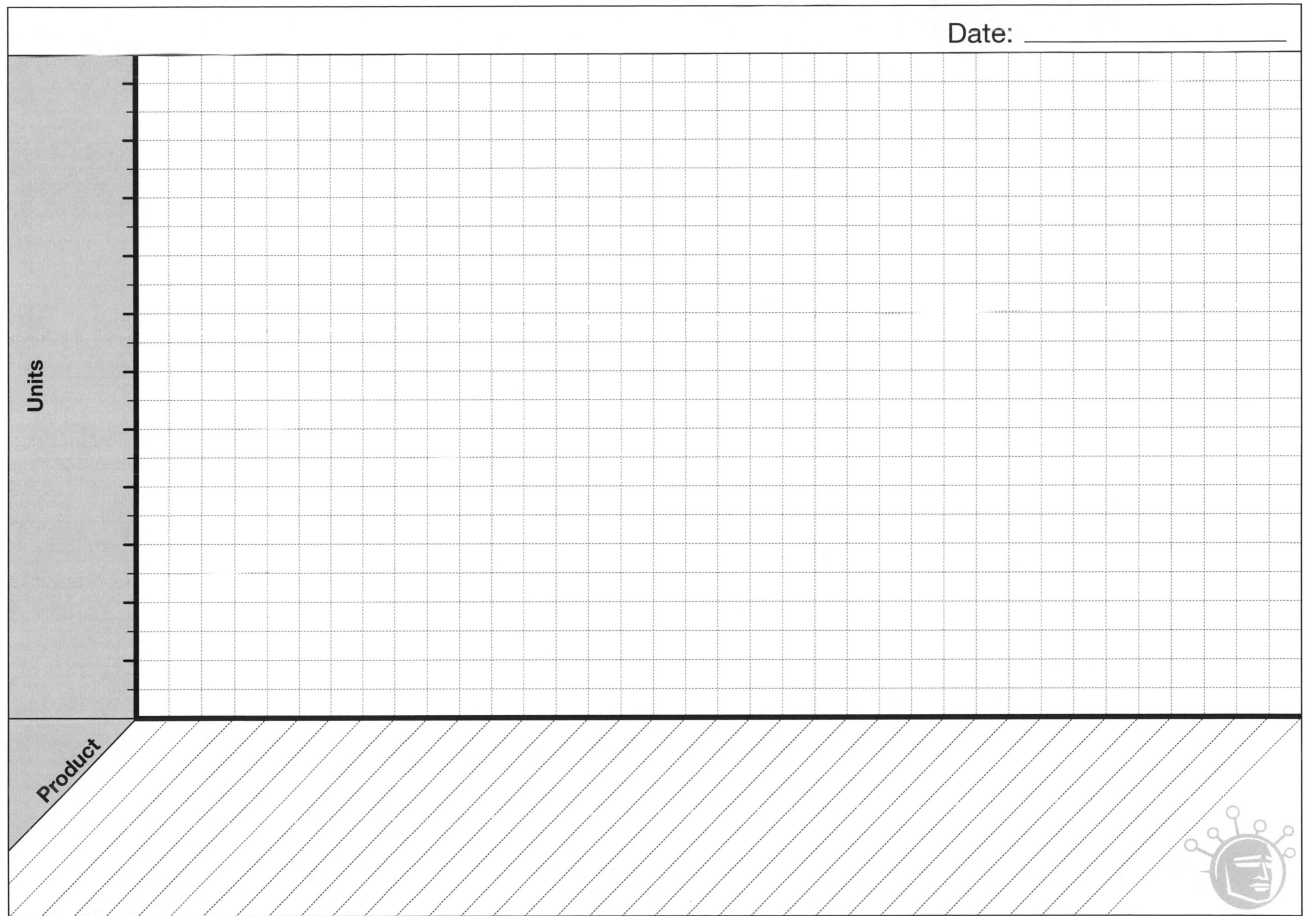

Date: _____

Units

Product

# Pareto Analysis

Date: _____

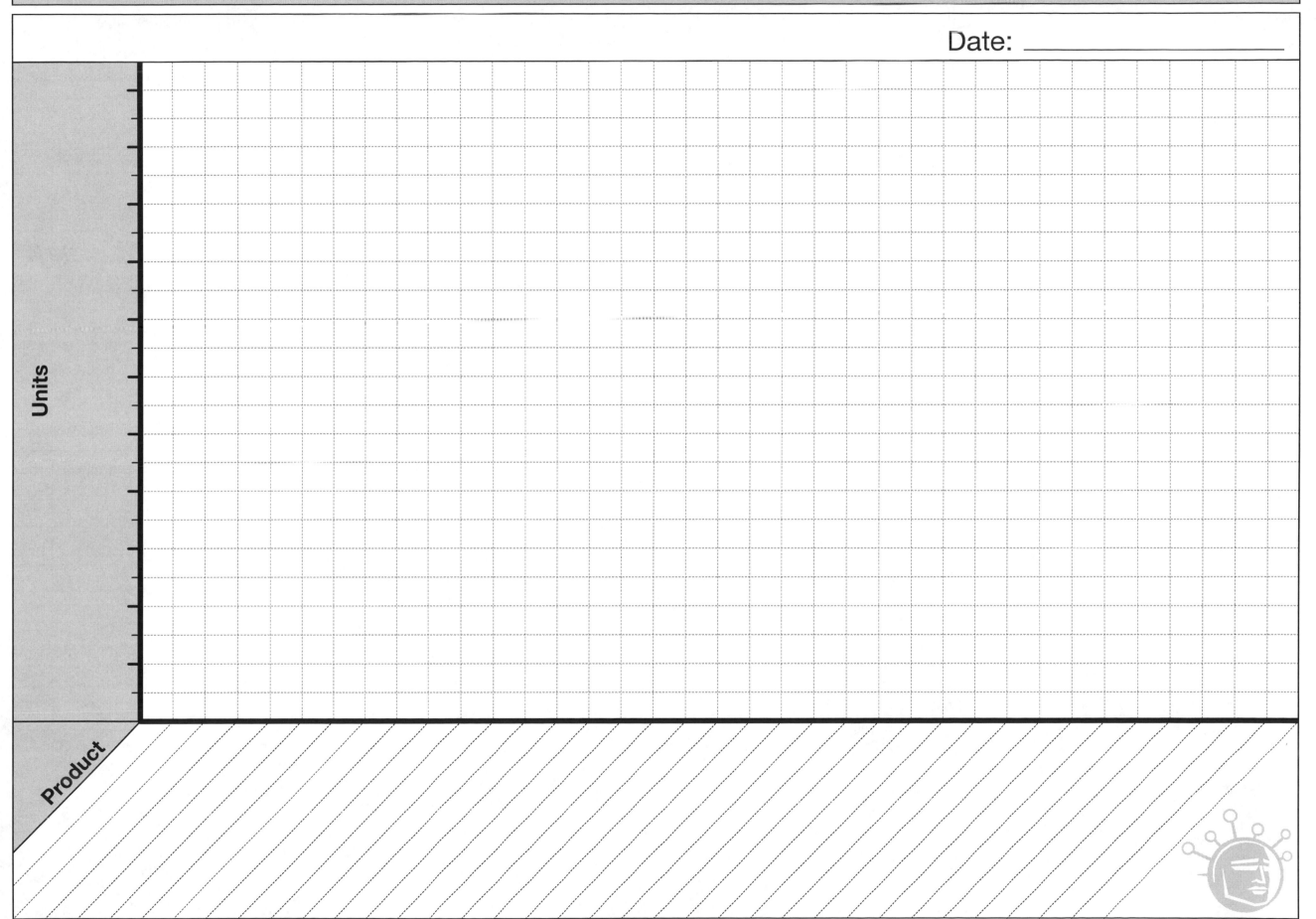

**Units**

**Product**

www.enna.com
www.productivitypress.com